RUNAWAYS

TEENAGE WASTELAND

TEENAGE WASTELAND

WRITER: BRIAN K VAUGHAN
PENCILS: ADRIAN ALPHONA &
TAKESHI MIYAZAWA
INKS: DAVID NEWBOLD & CRAIG YEUNG

COLOURS: UDON'S CHRISTINA STRAIN WITH BRIAN REBER
LETTERS: VIRTUAL CALLIGRAPHY'S RANDY GENTILE
COVER ART: JO CHEN
ASSISTANT EDITOR: MACKENZIE CADENHEAD
EDITOR: C B CEBULSKI

EDITOR IN CHIEF: JOE QUESADA
PUBLISHER: DAN BUCKLEY

PREVIOUSLY...

Teenager Alex Wilder and five other children always thought that their parents were boring Los Angeles socialites, until the kids witness the adults murder a young girl in some kind of dark sacrificial ritual. The teens soon learn that their parents are part of a secret organisation called The Pride, a collection of crime bosses, time-travelling despots, alien overlords, mad scientists, evil mutants and dark wizards.

After stealing weapons and resources from these villainous adults (including a mystical staff, futuristic gauntlets and a genetically engineered velociraptor named Old Lace), the kids run away from home and vow to bring their parents to justice. But when the members of The Pride frame their children for the murder they committed, the fugitive Runaways are forced to retreat to a subterranean hideout nicknamed the Hotel. Using the diverse powers and skills they inherited, the Runaways now hope to atone for their parents' crimes by helping those in need...

MARVEL presents: **RUNAWAYS: TEENAGE WASTELAND**

RUNAWAYS VOLUME 2: TEENAGE WASTELAND. Contains material originally published in magazine form as RUNAWAYS VOLUME 1 #7-12. Published by Panini Publishing, a division of Panini UK Limited. Mike Riddell, Managing Director. Alan O'Keefe, Managing Editor. Mark Irvine, Production Manager. Marco M. Lupoi, Publishing Director Europe. Brady Webb, Reprint Editor. Melanie Wilson, Designer. Office of publication: Panini House, Coach & Horses Passage, The Pantiles, Tunbridge Wells, Kent TN2 5UJ. Tel: 01892 500 100. Copyright © 2003, 2004, 2007 by Marvel Characters, Inc. All rights reserved. No similarity between any of the names, characters, persons and/or institutions in this magazine with any living or dead person or institution is intended, and any similarity which may exist is purely coincidental. This publication may not be sold except by authorised dealers and is sold subject to the conditions that it shall not be sold or distributed with any part of its cover or markings removed, nor in a mutilated condition. Runaways, Cloak and Dagger (including all prominent characters featured in this issue and the distinctive likeness thereof) is a trademark of MARVEL CHARACTERS, INC. and this publication is under license from Marvel Characters, Inc. through Panini S.p.A. Printed in Italy. ISBN: 978-1-905239-76-4

How do you think we convinced everyone in California that *Alex* murdered the young woman *we* sacrificed?

You... you framed your own *son*?

Desperate times, Mr. Dean. For added measure, Alex has also been implicated in the "kidnapping" of the Hayes' girl.

And to broaden our dragnet even further, we implicated Nico Minoru and Gertrude Yorkes in these crimes as well.

But what about my child? Who's looking for *her*?

We didn't want civilians to be able to connect all six of our families, so we opted not to involve your daughter or the Steins' son in this conspiracy.

We'll wait to create cover stories for their disappearances until enough news cycles have passed.

But how much time do we *have?* Chase took the Fistigons from our workshop. He's in possession of the most powerful gauntlets ever invented!

That's nothing, Stein. My Gertrude is running around with a bloody *velociraptor* genetically engineered to obey her every command.

What about *Nico?* My baby has the Staff of One now, the... the very mystic instrument that made the Dread Dormammu tremble!

You don't seriously think they'll use those weapons *against* us, do you? I mean, we're their *parents.*

10

Don't be *naive* Frank. Our children watched us slay an innocent girl in a damn *occult ceremony*. They've already *attacked* some of us.

To them, we're probably no different than the ridiculous "super villains" they see on the evening news.

But we *are* different! We're... we're *heroes*! We've dedicated our *lives* to making this world a better place for those kids!

Well, at least *one* of our brood believes you, dear. I found an unsigned note that one of them left behind... says they understood why The Pride did what it did, says they'll always be *loyal* to us.

Maybe that's true, but we can't just sit around and wait for whoever this *mole* is to contact us. It's imperative that we use all of our resources to *find those kids*.

Agreed.

There is nothing more dangerous than the wide-eyed idealism of *youth*. Frightened and confused as they may be...

...I have no doubt that our children are plotting to *overthrow* us even as we speak.

Molly, get off of Gert's dinosaur!

You're gonna hurt yourself!

And stop using the word "freaking" so much. It's freaking me out.

Arsenic says I can use any words I want to now, Alex. She says I don't have to do anything my *Mom and Dad* told me to do ever again.

First of all, her name is *Gertrude*, not "Arsenic". And secondly--

Gertrude is my *slave name*, Alex.

You can keep calling yourself whatever your evil parents named you, but the rest of us are *starting over*.

Right, Bruiser?

Right, Arsenic.

Aren't codenames supposed to be *cooler* than your actual names?

Hey, do I really not have to finish fifth grade?

Nope, school's out forever, kid.

That is *awesome!*

Gert, you can't *say* stuff like that! We're Molly's *guardians* now! We can't just--

Settle, big man. Do you really think I'm happy that I traded a future full ride at Mount Holyoke for life in a dilapidated *hotel*... much less a dilapidated hotel that fell down a *mineshaft*?

The kid's *eleven.* I'm not going to lie to her, but if we don't give her *something* to feel good about, the enormity of this whole messed-up situation will crush her like--

Lucy in the Sky and Talkback, reporting for duty, sir!

I'm in hell. My parents already killed me, and I'm in hell...

How's the code-breaking going, brother?

Slowly but surely.

I translated some of the first chapter, but I think it's mostly historical stuff. Whoever wrote this thing keeps talking about these weird six-toed giants called *Gibborim.*

Yeah, I'm pretty sure I've heard that word before, but I'd need a good search engine to confirm it.

Guess we're S.O.L. without D.S.L.

How about you, Chase? You and Karolina hide our wheels somewhere?

Yep, in *plain sight.*

I stole the plates off a Honda Civic and switched them with the ones on my van. It'll be months before that dude notices he's got the wrong license on his car.

Wait. *What?*

I warned you, send him to sell our cow and he'll come back with *magic beans...*

15

Listen, our parents' stormtroopers are looking for a white van with our plates, right? But now, if the cops see our ride and run the license, it'll come back totally clean, no red flags or nothing.

Trust me, I read it in this true crime book. Works every time.

Speaking of *dim bulbs*, did Lucy in the Sky just drop a few watts?

Oh, you mean my glow?

Yeah, Talkback noticed that I lose some of my intensity at night.

I figure blondie here gets her alien powers from the *sun*, like a solar-powered calculator, but bigger... and worse with numbers.

Hey, who are you calling *bigger*, Mr. Hand?

Sexual tension.

Gross.

That reminds me, has anyone seen--

My *staff!*

My staff is... is *gone*.

That creepy magic wand of yours?

You probably just misplaced it, Nic-- er, *Sister Grimm*. Took me about an hour to find my *off-switch* bracelet this morning.

There must be a million rooms in this funhouse.

Alex, it feels like I have something in my eye, but instead of my eye, it's... it's my *soul* or my--

I don't want to scare you, Nico, but when your mom stabbed you with that thing, it sorta disappeared into your *chest*, right?

Is there any chance when you went to sleep, your body, you know... *reabsorbed* it, or--

Can you guys make out later, please?

I'm freaking *starving*.

Food can wait, Molly. We haven't even figured out our next move against The Pride, and now Nico has something *inside* of her.

Well, at least *one* of us does. I'm with Bruiser. We haven't eaten in, like, twelve hours.

Maybe he's right, Alex. I'm... I'm probably just hungry.

Either way, what are we supposed to do? Call *Domino's*?

We can't use our credit cards or make ATM withdrawals without alerting the entire world to our whereabouts, and we only have nineteen bucks between us in cash.

Dude, your parents' fancy-pants lifestyle has made you *soft*. Nineteen bucks is enough to buy six people a *feast* at the local Circle A.

Fine. But if we're leaving the Hostel, we're going as a *group*. I don't want you coming back with any more magic beans.

Magic *what?*

Gert, stay here and keep an eye on Molly, will you?

Hey, why do I have to stay? I'm a *mutant*, 'member? I'm stronger than all you guys combined!

Don't worry, kid, if they forget to bring back Slim Jims for us, Old Lace here will teach them a lesson about the *food chain*.

RRRRRR

18

24

You two, get down on the ground and--

Back **off**, brat!

UHN!

ALEX!

It's not *your* hideout, it's *our* base. Besides, Chase, if we turn our backs on this kid, how are *we* any better than our--

Whoa, don't use my real name around this dude!

Talkback, be *nice*.

Why should I? This freak and his two pals just tried to knock over the Circle A! At *gunpoint!* We should leave him for the pigs!

No, please! I told you, those were my *parents!* They *made* me come with them! They're... they're *evil!*

Sound familiar?

That's *his* story. Why should we believe him?

Look into his *eyes*, Talkback. He's obviously been through the same stuff we have.

Five-oh! Everybody, West Wing!

WOOOOWOOOOWOOOO

32

"West Wing?"

Walk fast, talk fast. You have to learn to speak "Alex" if you're gonna run with the Children of the Damned...

Hold on. All of *your* parents are evil, too?

Lucy in the Sky, give him the Cliffs Notes.

Six of us ran away from home after we found out that our parents are part of this sick secret society called The Pride... and I mean *bad* sick, not cool sick.

They framed us for a murder we didn't commit, but we're using the powers and weapons we took from them to try and *help* people.

Wow, you're... you're like a junior version of the A-Team.

What's an A-Team?

Sorry, guess my interests are a little more... *retro* than yours.

How *old* are you guys, anyway?

Well, *Bruiser* is our youngest. She's eleven. She's back at The Hostel with Arsenic, who's fourteen or fifteen, I think.

Alex, Sister Grimm and I are all sixteen.

Oh, same here.

Believe it or not, Talkback up there is the elder statesman of our crew.

Yeah, I remember sixteen...

WOOOOOOOOOOOOOOO

...back when life was *simple.*

35

Huh, wonder why I didn't accidentally conjure up a bunch of birds *that* time? Maybe I can't cast the same spell *twice?*

How...?

She's pretty hardcore, huh? Sister Grimm is actually the daughter of two *sorcerers.*

What kind of bad guys are *your* parents, Topher? Androids? Demons? *Android demons?*

Um, none of the above, really. See, they both work-- *worked*-- for this power company in Sacramento.

There was some kinda accident at the plant, and when they got caught in the blast, they turned super-fast and super-strong, but also, you know... totally *nuts.*

They got fired 'cause they were too unstable to work, so they started robbing stores for cash.

Jeez, didn't they get workers' comp or anything?

I... I don't know. They just said they'd *kill* me if I didn't help them. And now they're out there somewhere, sick and confused, and... and I don't know what to--

Don't worry, Toph. You can crash at our place until the heat dies down, and I'll help you find your mom and dad first thing tomorrow morning.

It's like they teach you in first grade, if you ever lose your parents in a public place, just stay calm...

...they're bound to turn up soon.

Would you like a snack, Geoffrey?

I came down to fix myself some warm milk, and noticed that the neighbors had left a *bundt cake* on our porch.

"We were so sorry to hear about Alex on the news, but everyone in the neighborhood knows that your son is innocent, and you are all in our prayers."

Prayers. Lord, I sometimes forget what a pack of *imbeciles* we're surrounded by.

Well, I just got a late-night gift of my own.

The Pride's operative in Robbery/Homicide e-mailed me a few minutes of surveillance footage taken earlier tonight.

Really? What is it?

An answer to our prayers.

That's Alex! Where... where was this taken?

A convenience store in Los Feliz.

The kids are still in *California*? I thought they'd be halfway to *Canada* by now!

Do we know who they're fighting here?

A trio of thieves... new players. Whoever they are, they certainly didn't request a permit from The Pride to rob stores in *our* city.

Regardless, if the children have opted to start playing crimefighter, it's more imperative than ever that we find them quickly...

...before some two-bit hood makes an *example* out of them.

Home again, home again...

WHOA! This place is the--

RARRRRRRR

39

AHHH! WHAT IS IT?!

Oh, my God!

Where's Arsenic?!

HELP ME!

I'm here! I'm here!

Gert, call off your raptor!

I'm trying! Old Lace... she's not listening to my thoughts!

Then think harder, *Arse!* She's, uhh, too heavy to budge!

Says you, wimpster...

Scooch.

Old Lace, play *nice!*

See, she wasn't trying to hurt anybody. She just likes roughhousing.

Isn't that right, you big silly-head?

RRRRRRR

So, you guys bring back burritos?

Topher, this is *Gert*, whose manners are only slightly better than her *pet's*.

My *name* is... never mind.

Tell me, Never Mind, does that thing always try to eat guests?

Dunno. You're our first.

Topher is one of us, Arsenic. His parents are *eeeevil*.

If that's our only criteria for admission, this cave is gonna fill up *fast*.

Come on, Topher, I'll give you the nickel tour of the joint.

Yeah, I think I'll join you.

That's okay, Alex. I've got it.

Told you this was a bad idea, bro...

Hey, can you guys do me a favor?

If Topher asks about my *powers* or whatever, could you please not mention that I'm, you know...?

An alien?

Shh! I don't want to make him any more freaked out than he already is, okay?

Topher doesn't need to know I'm not... not from this *planet.* If he says anything, just tell him I'm a *mutant.*

Why? You know we'd accept you even if you were from *France,* Karolina! You shouldn't be--

God, I'm just asking you to do *one thing,* Chase!

You don't have to be such a...

Forget it, it's late.

I'm going to bed.

Man, this is just like the Real World... only *real.*

Nico, you're *bleeding*!

Did... did my parents *hurt* you?

Oh, this? No, it's nothing. I... I cut *myself*.

Why?

Actually, it's... complicated.

It's all right, Nico.

My ex-girlfriend was a *cutter*. She made me read this book, so I know all about having anger that you can't express, and turning it inwards when--

Topher, I cut myself because shedding my own blood is the only way to free the ancient magical weapon that my witch of a mom somehow trapped inside my *body*.

Oh.

But now that you mention it, I *am* sorta angry...

I'm sorry, did I--

No, it's just, there's kind of *someone else*. I don't think we're exclusive or anything yet, but we... we *kissed*, right after all of this started happening.

You and Talkback?

Eww, no! *Alex*.

Really? I mean, he seems like a great guy... but not exactly the kind of boy I picture being your *type*.

He's not. Not exactly. But we've both been through the same unbelievable experience, like two people who survived a plane crash together or something, right?

There aren't a lot of guys out there who understand what it's like to discover that the people who got you a *clown* for your seventh birthday are actually *super-villains*.

Well, for what it's worth... there's one more now.

Thanks, Topher. But I'm afraid I... I still can't kiss you.

Don't be afraid, Nico.

Why...?

Topher, *stop.*

This... this isn't right.

But you kissed me *back.*

I'm sorry, I... I don't know why.

My brain has been going in so many different directions since--

⸮ahem⸮

Everything okay up here?

Alex?

Yeah, uh, everything is--

Actually, I was just about to leave.

Topher, wait!

I should really get some shut-eye, Nico. My parents have had me on the run ever since their accident, and--

Fine, you can take a room in the *east* wing.

Nico, you and I need to *talk*.

POW!

Check it out, Arsenic! I've been practicing with my old man's gloves, and now I can, like, totally mold my flames into anything I imagine!

And I see you've imagined a *square*.

Very creative, Talkback.

That was called the *opening act*, dude.

Now comes the *real* rock...

SHA-BAM!

GAHHH!

FWOOM

Did you *see* that?! It was some kind of... of flaming monkey!

It wasn't a *monkey*, new kid. It was a *blazing samurai*.

And... you... you *made* that?

Is the new kid slow or something?

Hey, I have a *name*, you know.

Topher isn't a name, it's a *meat substitute*.

You're not *serious*, are you? I'm practically the only one with a normal name in this entire--

Dial it down, boys. You'll wake Sleeping Beauty.

HNNNNK... SHOOOOOOOO...

Good luck. The last time Bruiser used her mutant mojo, she sawed logs like that for *hours.*

Speaking of which, it's almost three in the morning. When do the *rest* of you... rest?

I saw my parents kill a girl, and then I found a dinosaur in my basement.

I haven't slept in *four days.*

Yeah, now that I'm kicking it without a curfew, I've been trying to come up with a dream schedule.

I figure I'm gonna stay up until seven A.M. every day, maybe catch the first hour of Stern before punching out, then sleep until, like... what would nine hours of Z's take me up to?

Well, if we're looking for my mom and dad tomorrow, I think I'm gonna try to get some sleep now.

See you guys later, I guess.

Hey, new kid.

What?

Don't worry about your folks.

We'll find 'em. I promise.

I don't know what to say, Alex.

You've been so sweet to me, and I've been acting like a total--

Nico...

No, you have to hear this.

I just did something completely awful, and you deserve to--

Nico, I already know that you and Topher kissed.

You... you do?

HOW?

Oh, our first night in the Hostel, I found this *secret room* next door. It's sorta like those passageways in my parents'--

You've been *spying* on me?

What?

NO!

I mean... not before just now.

And I wasn't spying. I was keeping an *eye* on you.

I thought Topher seemed like an okay guy, but if this stuff with our parents has taught me anything, it's not to--

I can't believe I *trusted* you!

Me?!

You know what, maybe I'm *glad* I kissed Topher.

Where are you--

⟨*AWAY*⟩

Nico?

HNNNNK... SHOOOOOOOO...

CHUH... ZZZZNNN...

Kill me.

Gert!

My *name* is--

Have you seen Nico?

You mean Sister Grimm?

Enough with the stupid names already!

When are you going to *grow up*?

Sorry, Peter Pan.

I thought not growing up was the whole *point* of this little club.

Never mind.

I'll find her *myself*...

60

Hello?

Anybody in here?

Oh, hi, Topher.

Sorry, didn't mean to intrude.

I've been trying to find a place to sleep, but every room looks like it's about to *collapse* in this wing.

Well, you can hang in here.

If you want.

Thanks, uh... sorry, is it *Lucy*?

Sort of. My real name is Karolina, but I started calling myself Lucy in the Sky 'cause...

I don't know.

It's stupid, I guess.

61

Uh...

I just want to feel normal, you know?

I want something to feel the way it's *supposed* to feel.

Karolina?

What are you *doing?*

Oh, great...

This isn't... I don't even know what's going **on**.

I was just trying to help Karolina deal with the fact that she's a **mutant**, and--

Oh.

Is **that** what she told you she is?

Nico, please!

She's not a **mutant**, Topher, she's an--

NO!

GWUHHH!

What is *wrong* with you?

Me?! You're the one kissing *my* guy!

Your guy? What about Alex?

How many guys do you *have*?

Get off, *jerk!*

I'm not the jerk, *you're* the--

RAAWAAAR

≷nnn≷

Nico and I figured out that her body *reabsorbs* her staff after every couple of uses. Just let her catch her breath and--

Get... get away from me.

But--

I... I have to get out of this place.

Nico, hold up!

Yeah, wait for--

Alex, maybe you should give her some space.

But I... I...

Carry a torch for her? Noted.

But it's like they say, if you love something...

"...set it free."

THE WILDER FAMILIES
MAIL

Any progress, dear?

Some.

The rest of The Pride and I have been attempting to identify the three unregistered rogues who attacked our children.

So far, all we know is that at least two of the trio appear to possess augmented strength, speed, and some degree of invulnerability.

Well then, they're most likely *mutants*, no?

That's precisely what I was about to ask the good Dr. Hayes.

It's possible, Wilder, but not likely.

My pureblood union notwithstanding, it's extremely rare to encounter more than one mutant with the exact same power.

These lowlifes probably just stumbled onto a cursed artifact or... or *radioactive meteorite*. You know, the usual.

You see, I'm not really sixteen years old. I was born at the turn of the century.

You're *four*?

Huh? Oh, no, *last* century. In 1900.

Eww! And I *kissed* you?

Cute.

Yeah, I got turned when I was your age. Made a small fortune in stocks after the Depression, then lost it all after the dot-com crash.

Holding up all-night liquor joints is a drag, but I've grown accustomed to a rather *expensive* lifestyle over the decades, you know?

So all that stuff you told us...

...was a *lie*? Yeah, pretty much.

I didn't want to get hauled off to jail because of some wannabe super-kids, so I made up that sad sack story about my mom and dad being *evil*.

And I *knew* you'd wolf down whatever broken-home bull I fed you.

If I've learned one thing in my long life, it's that angst-ridden brats like you *always* have parent issues.

78

You're lying. You have some kind of... of *hypnotic stare.* That's why we've all been acting so strange around you.

No, you've been acting so strange because you're *teenagers.* You're stupid, predictable, and easy to manipulate.

But *you,* you at least have *spunk.* That's why I'm going to *turn* you... and let you help me kill your *friends.*

No...

Too bad that scary magic wand is still trapped inside your perky little chest, huh? How are you going to *stop* me?

More importantly, why would you *want* to? I mean, I can give you *immortality.*

Besides, it doesn't look like you spend much time in the *sun* as is.

I... I don't want to be *evil.*

Becoming a vampire doesn't change who you are.

Growing up does that, letting the naiveté of adolescence be washed away by the cold hard water of life.

Trust me, when you've seen as much of *"humanity"* in action as I have, you start to realize that we're all just a bunch of animals.

And that means it's eat... or be eaten.

Someday, you'll understand.

When blood is shed...

...let the Staff of One emerge!

SHUNK!

AHHHHH!

OWW! *Man...* will you look at that. It went clean through me and out the other side!

But...

Sorry, kid. Whedon got it wrong.

Stakes don't kill vampires, they just give us *heartburn.*

And what do you know, I'm already on the mend.

See, the only thing that can off me is *sunlight...* and unfortunately for you, that's about three hours away.

Hey, Toph!

You're off the team.

KAFWOOM

Alex!

I'm sorry, I... I came looking for you because I was *jealous*, and I know it was wrong but I--

I love you!

I love you, too. Can you walk?

No, I can *run*. Come on!

Hurry! He heals fast!

So Topher's a... a *vampire*? Vampires are *real*?

Unless we're all having the exact same *nightmare*...

83

Where's Karolina?

Still upstairs, I guess. Why, what's going on?

It's Topher. He's a... a monster. *Literally.*

Say what? He's part of *The Pride*?

No, I don't think he works for our parents, but he's bad. *Very* bad.

I knew it. Old Lace smelled something funny on that guy the second he set foot in here.

RRRRRRR

Well, look who came crawling back.

87

Old Lace. **SIC HIM.**

No need to play possum with this thing anymore, huh?

I've already learned all of your *weaknesses.*

Hup!

Uhf! Hey, Gert? Do you know what really killed all the dinosaurs?

To happy endings then...

GAH!

What the...?

Sunlight. Your blood burns like...

I can't believe you hell creatures were idiotic enough to steal from establishments on *our* turf.

Please, we... we told you, we don't know *where* your kids are!

They took off with The One Who Fathered Us!

The other vampire? He's with our *children*?

He... he *was*. Topher was *slain* last evening. We... we can *sense* when we lose one of our bloodline.

They're telling the truth, Dale.

Fine.

End it, Mr. Minoru.

With pleasure.

NOOOOOO!

Is it possible? Could our offspring have *murdered* one of these things?

You feeling it, too?

Indeed...

Pride.

But don't confuse us with the *junkies* you deal with every night, Lieutenant Flores.

The experimental pharmaceuticals that gave us our powers over light and darkness were *forced* on us by evil men...

Lowlifes who preyed on the fact that me and Cloak were helpless little runaways.

Since that day, Dagger and I have vowed to help *all* children in need.

Swell, 'cause we could sure use a hand finding a few *runaways* of our own.

Molly Hayes.

You say this girl was kidnapped by *other* kids?

Yeah, three teenage runaways... Alex Wilder, Nico Minoru and Gertrude Yorkes.

Although there's a chance that, uh, *more* kids might be involved, too.

Well, there's nothing *"typical"* about these runaways. Before they went *AWOL* with *Molly,* they *murdered* an innocent girl.

Odd. In our experience, adolescents are rarely abducted by their own kind.

And typical runaways don't take off in *groups,* not unless they have similar experiences with seriously messed-up home lives... abusive parents and stuff like that.

And to make matters worse, we think a few of these freaks may have some kind of creepy *powers.*

Er, no offense, of course...

And I assure you, Dagger and I would not have come to your wretched city if we did not feel strongly about this case.

Don't mind Cloak.

East Coast/Left Coast rivalries die hard.

Please... I wouldn't have asked you two to travel all the way from New York if I didn't think you were the Hayes girl's last hope.

So, ah, what happens now?

We do what we do, Lieutenant.

Don't call us...

...we'll call you.

BEEEEEP BOP

TIEMENS

Calling....

Mr. Wilder?

Yes, I have good news, sire. The Pride may be one step closer to having its *offspring* back...

Well, *this* bites.

Keep it down, Chase. I'm a few chapters away from deciphering the *origin* of The Pride. That might help us figure out what their *next* move will be.

So what, Alex? Even if you *do* decode our parents' big book of evil, it's not like we're gonna be able to *stop* them.

Yeah, *they're* twelve of the most dangerous super-villains on the planet, and *we* almost got decimated by a sixteen-year-old *kid*.

He wasn't a kid. He was a *monster*.

Whatever! I'm sick and tired of moping around this dump! We have all of this... this *power*. We should be doing something with it, something *good*!

Yeah, like freeing all the turtles at Sea World...

PAFT

Nico, if we leave the Hostel now, we risk being found.

The risk is the same if we stay in one place forever, Alex... maybe greater.

Besides, you're the one who said that we should use this stuff we took from our parents to start making up for all the *suffering* they've caused.

I know, but I can't risk anyone else getting hurt... not after what almost happened to Karolina.

I'm... I'm *okay*, Alex. Really.

But I would feel a lot better if I could, you know, punch a bad guy in the face or something.

What are we supposed to do, just head out and *look* for trouble?

We can go on patrol... like the *Guardian Angels!*

We don't have to take on terrorists or anything yet. We can start small, purse-snatchings and crap.

Well... I suppose we need to make a supply run anyway.

Gert, you can stay here with Molly?

You can't leave us *alone*, Alex!

What if more *monsters* show up?

107

The kid's got a point.

I'm not sure Old Lace and I could survive any more *ampires-vay.*

All for one and one for whatever then.

Fine, you can tag along, Molly, but under *no circumstances* will you be permitted to leave the van. Got it?

Yes! We finally get to wear our costumes!

I'm the only one who made a costume?

And? Spit it out, mutant.

We're talking about full and total *retcon*.

When we are inevitably reunited with our children, my husband and I will *erase* all knowledge of these unfortunate events from their memories.

Mind-wiping? Don't be *insane!* That procedure leaves half of its subjects totally *brain dead!*

We believe *our* daughter is strong enough to survive the process, Yorkes. Is *yours...?*

Ladies and gentlemen, this debate is not worth having until our young ones are *found.*

Which is where *I* come in.

I believe most of you are familiar with Lieutenant Flores, one of our operatives in the *LAPD*.

Thank you, sire. I apologize for interrupting your gathering, but I didn't want to risk sharing this development over an open line.

I was watching the surveillance tape of your children trying to stop that convenience store robbery a while back, and I got to thinking--

Do any of you earthlings ever get to the *point*?

I got to *thinking,* what's the best way to find a bunch of missing teenage do-gooders?

With *other* runaway super heroes, right? Takes a thief to catch a thief, and all that.

So I had a pal in the NYPD put me in touch with these *Cloak and Dagger* characters, and--

You brought vigilantes?

To *our* town?

May I see your service revolver, Lieutenant?

Um, what fo--

BLAM

AHHHHHH!

MY KNEE!

Good Lord, if the *Gibborim* find out what we've done... This has to be taken care of *yesterday*.

Obviously, Dale. But *how*?

No more back channels, no more surrogates...

It's time to get our hands dirty.

Heh. *"Stark Naked"*.

We should get some kinda *award* for this.

Finally... a crime in progress.

What, defacing an ad for some evil corporation that's in bed with the military industrial complex?

That's not a crime, it's a *public service*.

Come on, Arsenic! This is the first action we've seen all night. We're gonna run outta *gas* before we find something better to fight!

Knock yourself out, Talkback, but I'm not going to help you guys play *junior fascists*.

Should I put my costume on *now*, Lucy in the Sky?

Um, sure, Bruiser... as long as you promise to stay in here and help Arsenic and Old Lace guard our wheels, okay?

Awwww, what a *rip!*

Quiet, team.

Let's get into character.

113

Who's to blame for this, Tandy?

For what?

Children killing children. Every year, it feels as if we see more and more of it.

I don't know, Ty.

But kids have been doing awful things to each other since the *Children's Crusade*, so maybe it's just...

What is it?

Something caught my eye. A *glimmer*.

How far?

Follow me.

I'll light the way.

x

114

AHH!

OYE!

Leave now, or she'll be popping *spleens* instead of paint cans.

Nah, son, the only thing popping 'round here's gonna be a *cap* in your mutie--

What is this, a bad remake of West Side Story?

I hate when people mess with the *classics.*

Capa y Daga!

Don't... don't hurt us, yo.

Piece is just a *water pistol*... see?

Vándalos.

Desaparecer o sufrir.

Alex Wilder and Nico Minoru?

You're coming with us.

How... how do you know our names? If you work for our *parents*, you can--

DROP THE WEAPON!

UHN!

Sister Grimm!

Everybody, chill!

I... I read about these two on the Bugle's website. Arm & Hammer or something. They're *good guys*, B-list heroes from New York!

B-List?

"Popularity isn't a concern", hu

L.S.D., you take tall dark and ugly! I'll get the chick!

Chas no!

Flame on, *skank!*

What did you call me?

Leave us *alone!*

Your light is my sustenance, girl.

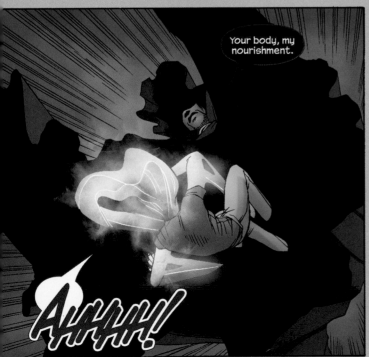

Your body, my nourishment.

AHHHH!

Hope you saved room for seconds, partner.

It's so... so *cold!*

Alex, help m--

Stop it!

I don't know what you've been told, but it's *wrong!* We're not killers, we're... we're just like you!

Tell it to Judge Ito, Wilder.

Don't you see what this is? Two groups of super heroes meet, have a stupid misunderstanding, then fight?

This routine was old when we were *born!* We don't have to--

Be silent, murderer... and enter the fold.

Nice.

We didn't take down *Stilt Man* that fast.

Hn.

Uh-oh, I don't like the sound of *that* grunt.

My relationship with the Darkforce Dimension has been... *temperamental* since my original abilities were restored during our misadventure in *Cleveland.*

Still, the four within my cloak's shadowy realm... I sense no stain of *blood* on their souls.

What are you saying? They're *not* murderers?

It is possible.

And yet, in one of them, I do recognize a powerful *darkness,* a--

Hey, Desdemona!

What the--?

You think *we* look weird?

What's with that slutty get-up, lady? Don't you have any *self-respect*?

Nope, but I've got *these*.

SHN

The one with the beast is Gertrude Yorkes, no?

Yeah, she's one of the brats who kidnapped the little Hayes girl.

By the way, kid, if you don't like *this* outfit...

...you should see my *old* one.

125

Old Lace,
now!

RAAARR

Thanks for
the cover,
O.L.

Is... is she
okay?

Yeah, just
hungry.

Um,
problem.

My powers,
they don't have
any effect on
animals or--

THWAP

Dagger!

UHN!

Easy, Old Lace.

She's just a skinny little thing.

We don't want to break her in *two*...

Child, if you have harmed her in any way, I will kill you with my own--

STOP FIGHTING!

Just let our friends out of your ugly *cape!*

Come on, I don't wanna have to rip up your bed sheets!

This is not a "sheet", girl. It is a *cloak*, a gateway to another realm permanently bonded to my very being.

Not even a *god* has the strength to rend it from my--

UMPH!

RAHHHH!

TY!

UHN!

Puh-puh-**please.**

Guh-guh-give it buh-buh-**back** to me.

I'm sorry! I thought you were another **monster.**

I didn't know you were a **stutterer.**

You made me ruh-ruh-**revert** to who I was when I fuh-fuh-**first** donned my cloak.

My mommy is a speech therapist. Maybe **she** can help you!

Bruiser, your parents are psychotic **super-villains.**

Oh, yeah.

I keep forgetting...

Super-villains?

What are you two *talking* about?

Yeah, our *folks*. The people who duped you into coming after us.

No, the *police* asked for our help.

Same diff. They're all in it together, part of something called "The Pride". They murdered a chick and framed *us* for the crime.

But the little girl you guys *kidnapped*...

How blonde *are* you?

That's Molly Hayes!

Aww! You ruined my secret identity!

See, we didn't *kidnap* anybody. We *rescued* her.

Oh, my God. Then your pals... *they're* innocent, too?

And now they're tr-tr-trapped in the Duh-Duh-Darkforce Dimension.

The *where* now?

Nnn.

Her knives... her knives showed me my sins...

Nico's delirious.

Chase, can you use your Fistigons to build us a campfire?

I... I think they're *busted*, dude.

It's our powers. They don't work here.

I'm not an *alien* in this place. I'm... I'm just a regular--

WHHOOOOOOOOOOO

What was *that*?

This isn't real!

It *can't* be!

It can't be...

What do you mean they're *lost*?!

When Molly ruh-ruh-ripped my cloak from me, she suh-suh-severed my connection to your friends.

It was an accident! I didn't know it was a *magic* cape!

Hold on, I have to wrap my brain around this.

This guy's outfit is like the mystical equivalent of a portal to the internet, but the server crashed, so before we can perform a *search,* we have to find a way to get it back online... *right?*

That was the worst analogy I've ever heard... but it gives me an idea.

My light daggers have a *purifying* quality. If I pump Ty full of them, I might be able to *repair* his link to Creepsville.

There's a duh-duh-danger of *overdose,* but it's our only huh-huh-*hope.*

Close your eyes, kiddies.

This is gonna be bright...

...but it might not be *pretty.*

GAH!

NO!

I didn't do *anything!* Why are they taking *me*?!

Nico, wake up! I don't think we're going to make it out of this, and I... I have to *tell* you something.

Alex, I *know.*

No, you *don't.*

Nico, I--

NYARRGH!

OOF!

Presto!

Everybody... in one... *piece*?

You. You sent us to *Hell*.

Hands off, Talkback.

We don't need any more meaningless punching.

Yeah, then what *do* we need?

The only thing our kind dreads...

Dialogue.

So this Lieutenant Flores jerk who put us on your scent...?

Yeah, sounds like he's an agent of The Pride, too. I'm sorry, they've got their fingers in *everything*.

We want our parents taken down *hard* for what they've done, but obviously, we're not quite Earth's Mightiest Heroes yet.

Speaking of which, I'm good friends with the Black Widow.

I'm sure she could put you in touch with Captain America and those guys, maybe send *them* out here to clean house.

Are... are? you serious? That would be *amazing!*

In the meantime, you children are clearly not safe in Los Angeles. You will come back to New York with us.

In *that* thing?

No offense, bro, but I'd sooner spend the night at Neverland Ranch.

137

I'm ashamed how often I agree with Chase, but I don't think I could survive another trip like that either.

Well, maybe we can stay in L.A. for a *little* longer, Nico... until the good guys are ready to pick us up in a Quinjet or whatever?

Pick you up *where*, exactly?

No way, sister! The last time we told someone about my hideout, they nearly *ate* us!

Chase, these guys are *heroes*.

So were my mom and pops, up until I found out they *weren't*.

Seriously, we don't know these cats from--

Enough. Cloak and Dagger have all the info they need to send the super-people after our parents.

They can assemble a posse in Manhattan, and we'll go back into hiding until our 'rents are in the slammer and the coast is clear.

Maybe that makes us cowards... but I *love* that plan. I don't think I have any fight left in me.

Hey, you guys are *anything* but cowards.

Me and Cloak didn't have *half* your guts and street smarts when *we* ran away from home.

Hn.

Well, I guess we should head back to our... place. Can we give you a ride somewhere or--

Thanks, Alex, but I think we'll rest here until we've gotten enough juice back for our jump to NYC.

You just keep taking good care of your team, okay?

Hang in there, Molly! This is all gonna be over soon!

Thanks! It was awesome to meet you, Cloak and Dazzler!

My *name* is...

I hate this city.

139

Dude, can we make a pit stop for some fish tacos or something?

Chase, we only have a few bucks left between us, and we *already* had dinner today.

I know, but I puked it up when we went through Ghost World back there.

Besides, Alex, we're about to be *rescued!* We don't need to store any more nuts for winter... spring's right around the corner!

Yeah, we *won* today! And Mom and Dad always let me eat out after I won at *soccer!*

Bruiser, your mom and dad--

No, Molly's right, Gert. We did okay tonight.

Let's *live* a little...

BZZBZZBZZ

What?

Lieutenant Flores?

Speak up, kid. You're mumbling. I can barely understand--

You're the dork who sent Cloak and Dagger after us, right? I'm surprised our parents haven't killed you yet.

Who... who is this?

141

Right now, I'm the only friend you've got.

You're one of their **children**, aren't you?

The Pride told me they might have a **mole** in your gang, but I didn't believe--

Quiet. I don't have long. I'm at a payphone outside some taco shack, and the others think I'm in the bathroom.

What do you--

Listen, Cloak and Dagger are on a rooftop in Van Nuys, but I'm not sure how much longer they'll be there.

Lieutenant, they **know** about The Pride.

How?

Doesn't matter. The only thing **you** should care about is cleaning up your mess.

But I'm stuck in the hospital! The Pride shot my **kneecap** off!

Do **something**... or the next bullet will probably be to your **brain**.

144